The Radiant Inventory

BOOKS BY CHRISTOPHER DEWDNEY

The Radiant Inventory

poems by

Christopher Dewdney

M&S

Canadian Cataloguing in Publication Data

Dewdney, Christopher, 1951-
  The radiant inventory

Poems.
ISBN 0-7710-2699-4

I. Title.
PS8557.E846R32 1988   C811'.54   C88-095058-7
PR9199.3.D48R32 1988

The Publisher would like to thank the Ontario Arts Council for its assistance.

Set in Simoncini Garamond by The Typeworks, Vancouver

Printed and bound in Canada

McClelland and Stewart
The Canadian Publishers
481 University Avenue
Toronto, Ontario M5G 2E9

The Radiant Inventory

Contents

THE SECULAR GRAIL

Radiant Inventory

The world has become
a spectacle of absence,
a radiant inventory.
The sunlight that falls
on the margin of the lake
nurtures a deficit
in its clarity, its violence.
These waves are items are
a description of themselves
in discourse with their changes
through time. The sand
is a finite texture of
self corruption. Everything
interpenetrating, extensile,
at once continuous and discrete.
This sunlight both sustains and erodes
the luminous surface of matter
the precise miracle of life.

Now that I have been opened
I can never be closed again.
The reflection of the sun on the waves
is a shining path to the horizon
a dazzling lucent shuttle
of unknowable complexity.
A cloud over the sun
momentary camera obscura.

And as I move towards resolution
the world abandons its detail
in a theatre at once dark & light
where life is a kind of joyous shade
a shadow over the sun
a dark radiance.

Depth Sounding, Lake Windermere

Suspended
        on the still surface of the night lake
we paddle silently towards the beach.
Its mysterious presence a kind of muteness, an assertion
equivocal to our liquid passage.
On the shore
a stand of birch
becomes a grove of fossil lightning
in the blinding silence
of a full summer moon.

Our paddles conspire purchase
in an invisible plane
glistening, imageless.
Each stroke leaving
two whirlpools,
        whispering vortices which zipper up
a single vocable.
Utterance from
the depths of the lake.

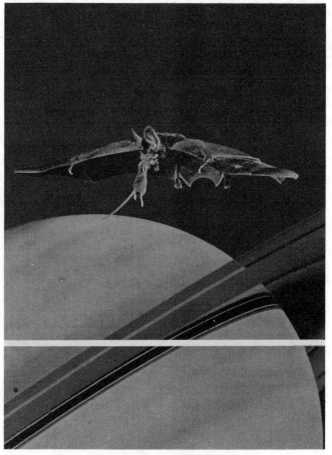

THE EVACUATION ZONE

This My Emissary

Sleep, come
unjoined with me.
I am radiant darkness,
a boundless prison
                    permeated with escape.
And what little the night recovers
is squandered at dawn.
For the heart has contrived a harm
borne of utter simplicity.

I have passed through the still eye of the storm.
I have seen the full moon in broken pine chiaroscuro
on the freshly fallen snow.
                    For the eye of the needle
is the still eye of the storm.
And when kneeling she wept
it was in the abject darkness
of total humiliation. This
my emissary
for the great silence
                    In her misery we know it.

Open Heart

for my father

The sweat on his forehead, beaded
into the white hair I stroked in I.C.U.
while reading his vital signs. A labour
so immense my father was a giant
breathing like a beached whale,
his heart too big for all of us.
His existence honed
to a single desperate thread.
                          Intensive care
an ozone delirium
of catheters & hissing oxygen
hallucinatory with panic.
                Then suddenly in agony,
his final crisis clinically illuminated
by the oblique November sun
a sacrifice
                tossed jerking down the temple steps
away from us.

(O yes. And now
an image of him,
an image of him
                    falling
like a silver coin lost
through a hole in the ice.

Winking dimly as it sinks
                              into the depths of the lake.
The spring ice he fell through
up to his armpits as a young man in Kenora.
An image of him
falling away from us
turning over & over, rigid,
like a doll, so completely
so totally
beyond
our will to bring him back.

Father
through all the others' eyes
by which I have seen you grow stranger
each one a little death,
I still know you
know your will a single curved muscle
a fine obsidian blade
suspended for an instant above the rapids
catching the sun like a fish
                              leaping
above the foam & spray
before it falls back
into the commotion
the background radiation
of the universe.

Shadows of Silence

There is a word
in the shadow of time. It
sounds as no surprise here
on the infinite brink
of our past.
If you listen carefully,
fill the instant with ears,
you can hear reality
echoing slightly
as it falls into
the relentless funnel of history.
Each of us
a single moment
growing older. Surrogate dreamers
in the shadow of thought.

Words
are the silence
at the heart of ideas
and the terrible truth
we turned crying from the mirror
to face
was simply
this prison of thought.

The Owls

We undress at the edge of the dark woodlot
and slip under the skin of the lake.
On the bottom of the pond
there is a dusky village the
dream of a child sleeping
in the back seat of a car.

Tonight even the owls
are dreaming on the wing,
soundless flickering stains in
the dark sanctum of night's night.
They break their predatory silence
with the eerie spectral address
of dream hunters.
The terrible beaks and claws of night.

All things here writhe, twist somehow as
ciphers in the dream's earthen logic.
Here at the eve of self where
we falter before each other's divinity
locked into our skin, distant
strangely & cruelly numb to the other.

Yet now, embracing underwater,
our bodies come unlocked and
we gush upwards, rising

from the dark lake
in a storm of music. And there
in the absolute theatre of night
we fuse, recover
the lost disorder of the stars.

Cascade Mountain

The mountain is a lunar terrain.
Not an icon
not a smooth symbol
but an aggregate of locales.
A vertical landscape containing
a thousand human domains.

Through the blue particulate haze
of a September noon
Cascade is a ragged
orogenetic stupa, an ancient portion
of planetary topography. Strata
canted up at an impossible angle
by prodigious tectonic labour,
the continent crumpling
at the edge of the ocean.

The scale astounds, each square mile
proffered to my eye.
Crags & valleys, spillways of boulders.
Such record, millions of days
the compressed gestures of oceans
imbedded in rock.
Its presence stuns, its mass
a silence of the soul, an indictment
as if we shared a secret, a profound &

prior union. Impassive, immutable calm
in our origin. I ignite in its focus
of mutual destiny. And at night
rounded in the darkness
it becomes a giant wave
frozen in the alchemy of midnight.
A blind tectonic leviathan
in momentary stasis.

The Radiant Inventory

Contents

THE SECULAR GRAIL

Radiant Inventory

The world has become
a spectacle of absence,
a radiant inventory.
The sunlight that falls
on the margin of the lake
nurtures a deficit
in its clarity, its violence.
These waves are items are
a description of themselves
in discourse with their changes
through time. The sand
is a finite texture of
self corruption. Everything
interpenetrating, extensile,
at once continuous and discrete.
This sunlight both sustains and erodes
the luminous surface of matter
the precise miracle of life.

Now that I have been opened
I can never be closed again.
The reflection of the sun on the waves
is a shining path to the horizon
a dazzling lucent shuttle
of unknowable complexity.
A cloud over the sun
momentary camera obscura.

And as I move towards resolution
the world abandons its detail
in a theatre at once dark & light
where life is a kind of joyous shade
a shadow over the sun
a dark radiance.

Depth Sounding, Lake Windermere

Suspended
        on the still surface of the night lake
we paddle silently towards the beach.
Its mysterious presence a kind of muteness, an assertion
equivocal to our liquid passage.
On the shore
a stand of birch
becomes a grove of fossil lightning
in the blinding silence
of a full summer moon.

Our paddles conspire purchase
in an invisible plane
glistening, imageless.
Each stroke leaving
two whirlpools,
              whispering vortices which zipper up
a single vocable.
Utterance from
the depths of the lake.

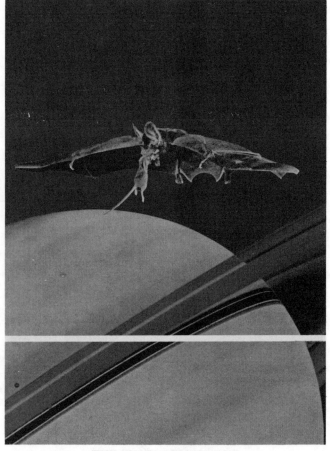

THE EVACUATION ZONE

This My Emissary

Sleep, come
unjoined with me.
I am radiant darkness,
a boundless prison
                permeated with escape.
And what little the night recovers
is squandered at dawn.
For the heart has contrived a harm
borne of utter simplicity.

I have passed through the still eye of the storm.
I have seen the full moon in broken pine chiaroscuro
on the freshly fallen snow.
                For the eye of the needle
is the still eye of the storm.
And when kneeling she wept
it was in the abject darkness
of total humiliation. This
my emissary
for the great silence
                In her misery we know it.

Open Heart

for my father

The sweat on his forehead, beaded
into the white hair I stroked in I.C.U.
while reading his vital signs. A labour
so immense my father was a giant
breathing like a beached whale,
his heart too big for all of us.
His existence honed
to a single desperate thread.
                      Intensive care
an ozone delirium
of catheters & hissing oxygen
hallucinatory with panic.
           Then suddenly in agony,
his final crisis clinically illuminated
by the oblique November sun
a sacrifice
              tossed jerking down the temple steps
away from us.

(O yes. And now
an image of him,
an image of him
                 falling
like a silver coin lost
through a hole in the ice.

Winking dimly as it sinks
                    into the depths of the lake.
The spring ice he fell through
up to his armpits as a young man in Kenora.
An image of him
falling away from us
turning over & over, rigid,
like a doll, so completely
so totally
beyond
our will to bring him back.

Father
through all the others' eyes
by which I have seen you grow stranger
each one a little death,
I still know you
know your will a single curved muscle
a fine obsidian blade
suspended for an instant above the rapids
catching the sun like a fish
                    leaping
above the foam & spray
before it falls back
into the commotion
the background radiation
of the universe.

Shadows of Silence

There is a word
in the shadow of time. It
sounds as no surprise here
on the infinite brink
of our past.
If you listen carefully,
fill the instant with ears,
you can hear reality
echoing slightly
as it falls into
the relentless funnel of history.
Each of us
a single moment
growing older. Surrogate dreamers
in the shadow of thought.

Words
are the silence
at the heart of ideas
and the terrible truth
we turned crying from the mirror
to face
was simply
this prison of thought.

Night Trains

A night train is a part of ourselves
on its way to another part of ourselves
in the darkside of consciousness.
A train is a state of things in transit,
a cartesian living-room passing through
a narrative geography.

The sound of wheels
on glistening steel rails
is a continuous ball-bearing glissando
a metallic rolling peal
interrupted staccato
by the seams in the tracks.
The engine gliding
on frictionless iron, both
machine and path part
of a single mechanism such
that passage is an illusory extension
in space. The labour
that keeps us here
roaring in my ears.

And in the mountains, the train whistle
is supernaturally sustained
by the still air of the valleys
an indulgence of the massif
to echo for full seconds in the
dream kingdom of the night mountains.

Halcyon July in Algoma

A month of such
cloudless blue days
that each morning the lake
was a celestial wound
an amber bowl of pectin
highlit with mazarine.
The clusters of offshore islands
interrupted this plain
like a frozen pod of granite dolphins,
their pink backs aligned
by a forgotten glacier.
                Cetaceans forever bound
                for the heart
                of the Wisconsin ice age.

And slowly, hypnotically
when the sun went nova each noon
a haunted stillness
enclosed our island. A
calm so lucid
that the flight of a single bird
through the resonant air
was a portentous event
of invidious design.

Each Other the Work

There is nothing
coincidental
about us, except
the ultimate
coincidence
of our meeting.
Our bodies
narrow margins of desire
against the stars.

The summer fields
we used to play in
before the
cruel intercession
of urban demographics.
As if I could imagine
a home this distant
in your arms.

But we meet again and
again
in the pale light
of mnemnos
something intangible
alighting
on my outstretched hand.

To be with myself
is to be faced
with you. The
magnolias in bloom,
windy pink flash
against a grey sky.
The love which springs
glistening from our work.

Jaguarundi

Two jaguarundi appear
at the river's edge. Terrestrial
otters. Their lank bodies
seamlessly insinuated
through the tall grass.

They move like pure intention,
familiars materialized
by your looking.
Drinking from the river
they seem to spring
without moving.
The jaguarundi's crouch
is a stroboscopic bridge
of potential leaps.

One turns & vanishes
leaving a residue its
signal libido.
The other still drinking
crouched & tensile,
sensing the heat
of nearby animals.

Then this one, turns,
disappears into the grass.

Merging with the dark grace
of an entire species
into the greenness
by the river.

Heatwave

Heatwave silence.
Time-wind in the
backyard maple.
A flock of sparrows
fills the tree
with cuneiform sound,
acoustically tempered by the heat.
As if they had transposed
the resonance of a cathedral
into the canopy of this
single immense tree.
A domed aviary, a museum with
its branches swaying
in the wind at the crest
of the hill.

After the birds leave
a single cicada calls out
from the centre of the tree.
Heralding the late afternoon,
its buzzing song is a
staccato incantation. Fulcrum
of the solar anvil.

Grey Wind, Grey Light

November is an abandoned landscape
of ubiquitous, intimate theatre.
It is the seasonless month
indistinguishable from March
or early December, an interlude
with no determining characteristics.
The gothic woodlots
are hieratic armatures
for the empirical, steel-grey
light of reason, illuminating
the flesh of the world.
The forests are the ruined
scaffolds of summer
nursing twilight in their heart.

November is a calm month, subject
to unnaturally warm & sunny days
though normally steeped
in a cool marine illumination.
The spectral lithography
of leafless forests.
University chestnut trees,
stoically presiding over
the circular litter of brown leaves.
This moody grey light
is a proscenium for love's
endless diorama. The late Pleistocene geography

a continuous undulating plain
of glacial artefacts.
The ice just below the soil
(High arctic sub-tropical Eocene,
the perma-frost gradually
freezing out paradise
on Axel Heiberg.)
The smooth grey trunks of the beech trees
are a muscular condensation
of the grey skies spreading like strata
over this radiant landscape
a boreal theatre benignly illuminated
with the tranquillity of devastation.
The rolling vista of low limestone hills
soft ridges and valleys &
sporadic clumps of junipers,
their opaque green greyness concentrating
and radiating the light
of this grey November afternoon.

Morraines gouged by highways,
the deep yellow ochre of sandy eskers &
dark blue glacial clay beneath.
A worn mammoth tooth at the edge
of a small river, indistinguishable
from the cobbles washed out
of the morraine. Viburnum bushes still green
across the river, as are the willows.
Limited regional tableaux of summer.
And flitting over the paths in the woodlot
are pale tan moths, the most unearthly

and hardiest of all. Their purposeful
faltering mating flights
in the cool air of forest clearings.
English ivy bright green on the
limestone walls of a country church,
Bach *orgelwerke* distant & within.

There is a licence in the abandoned hills,
a love at the end of time. The world becomes
a projection of pure mood
in the industrial illumination of November.
There is permission in this deserted world
the final fusion of anticipation and moment.
Deep emerald lawns against
the grey muted colours of the woodlot,
distant skyline of the city.
The forests are stripped of adornment
like a dismantled amusement park.

November is the future
we always thought we'd inhabit.
The endless sliding of featureless clouds a
planar strata scrolling over the horizon.

November is the month of polished metal,
of mat alloys. It is the month
of mammalian gloss, of quiet rain.
Tchaikovsky ponds misting in the twilit forest.
Month of reality, of children's calm
magical insight into interiority.

November grey afternoons and houses
leaking their darkness into the air
through second story windows.
The cool twilight of November evenings
the diffusion of outside & in.

By the river the cedars abide
rank after rank, gather the magic gloom
and stoically gesticulate
in the altered light of these grey afternoons.
The hawk a predatory funnel of vision
perched in the dead elm.

November is the light of miracle.
Its flat brilliance evokes
even the darkness within objects,
made newly strange in its radiance
It is a light of appraisal,
of evaluating diamonds.
It is the illumination of lucid eros
of explicit lust heightened
by the vicarious liberty of desertion.
November is the evacuation zone. The delighted
privacy & glow of satiety in the existential
incandescence of a vacant, anticipatory panorama.

It is the month of memory. We re-enact
the spectacle of summer, clothing boughs
in a mnemonic foliage that lingers
over the deserted landscape.

And then a warm south wind.
Leafless white branches of an apple orchard
under wild skies. The grey wind
spawns a perverse autumnal spring
warrant to our appalling, our enthralling sex
in the furrows of a freshly ploughed field
the cornstalks turned under &
sown with winter wheat.

EQUIVOCAL MERCIES

QUANTUM PHENOMENA, NORMALLY BELOW THE
THRESHOLD OF PERCEPTION, OCCASIONALLY MANIFEST
THEMSELVES TANGIBLY.

Points in Time

Two points stabilize two dimensional space. Three points stabilize a three dimensional object. Four points stabilize four dimensional space. A point is one dimension.

A point in motion is a line. A line in motion is a plane. A plane in motion is a solid. A solid in motion is time.

The quantum theory applies to time, which progresses in small pulses of very short duration. The universe exists as a phantom between pulses. The power of the phenomena existing in one pulse is enough to generate itself through the gap, the interval of non-being, into existence in the next pulse. An event or phenomenon loses a small parcel of energy each time it is propagated through the gap.

The universe exists and does not exist in regular, rapid succession.

A fixed point in time, or one quantum, stabilizes the continuum, which is how everything happens at once.

DNA is the selective mutational interface between cosmic noise and survival. Humans are the product of a phylogenic memory locked in one direction by DNA.

Now it is night and the clay bluffs are alive with thousands of tiny wriggling white mares. The sky is entirely composed of what appears to be a billion prismatic reflections, spectral smears. Each one the same device, a grinning monkey set guardant on a jackhammer. Its face a blur of verticality.

The Face-Fixers

The face-fixers wait on dark streets at night. If they see your face just once your soul is etched deeply into their plan of terror and insanity.

Fear moves fast in still water.

The face-fixers cannot fix on the receding back of a potential soul. Whole streets are sometimes set up in chains of them. One an old lady with a handbag, one a student fixing his bicycle, another an eleven-year-old girl just behind a hedge in the soft evening light. All turn to look at you and you must hide your face without attracting undue attention.

If your evasion techniques set up "eccentric behaviour" patterns there are two levels on which this behaviour is intercepted. On the first level, animals crazed with telekinetic fear will attack. You will have your pants ripped off by a German shepherd, tuberculoid owls will swoop into your face. The second level dovetails into a rehabilitation network, in this case policemen and psychiatrists who are actually face-fixers in disguise.

They rely heavily on the genetic and psychic damage wreaked while man perverted the evolution of domestic beasts.

The Incremental Geneology of Spring

The youngest spring, which is youth and sex incarnate, love's blossom, begins on January evenings. The clear sunsets of cold January days harbour the vernal spawn in the green margin between the sunset and the sky. Particularly above the vacant, windswept plazas on the outskirts of the city. In the deeper blue above the evening afterglow spring is present in a rarefied vapour.

Spring is deposited as a patina on the cliffs of apartment buildings glowing orange in the setting sun. The full moon ascending behind them, the violet eastern sky. Spring hides in any water that is fluid at these times.

In its crystalline state, spring survives being frozen in the subthermal clarity of January nights.

Video Marquee

It is a clear cool night in late summer. You are looking across a small creek at an old one-room cabin. The creek is two metres wide and has a small ramshackle wooden bridge across it, consisting merely of a ramp with no hand-railing.

The cabin has light coming through one window and a crooked stovepipe juts from the roof. A cosy sleepy feeling emanates from the cabin, though slightly unfamiliar, as if you were a child on your first night away from home. It is perhaps 2 or 3 A.M. Behind the cabin is a dense coniferous forest. The tops of the trees are silhouetted against the deep-blue sky, in which stars twinkle and a waning moon hangs.

This scene is the video marquee, the illustrated logo of a regional lateshow. It has been on for fifteen minutes without sound. Unattended station difficulties. You are twelve years old, watching a late movie on television at a cottage on the southeast shore of Lake Huron. Your friend has fallen asleep. It is a warm summer night and moths flutter around the light at the porch. You can hear the waves on the beach faintly. It is about 2 or 3 A.M. and a waning moon is suspended over the lake. Far north on the same shore a cabin sits near a small creek running into the lake. It is much cooler in the north and the cabin's windows are closed. Inside, a twelve-year-old boy and thirteen-year-old girl are masturbating each other, kneeling face to face on a couch bathed in the light of the television screen.

The Lateshow Diorama

Exploring the cold night of the lateshow diorama you come upon the outskirts of a small town, its boundary marked by an abandoned corrugated-steel hangar. The hangar is about a block long and sections of the roof are missing. The entire structure seems to consist only of girders and corrugated steel.

A guard dog, tethered at the far end of the hangar, barks. As you turn towards the first streetlights the sound takes on a distant, rusty quality. The motion of turning produces an unexpected time dilation as the interior of the hangar is transposed into the back of your head. A hollow glimpse of the stars and blue night sky through a tear in the ceiling. A gap to the stars as you turn now in imagination a cascade of motion as you turn in images of your tearing away from the image, the entrance, to explore the sleeping town.

As if you had left a trace, a phantom in time at which the olfactory dog continued to bark.

Portrait of the Soul in a Timeless Room

You are sitting up in bed in a room which is at once familiar and foreboding. The only sound is the rustling of your sheets as you change position. Along the wall are two windows through which you can see a night sky with huge, luminous stars. In the fireplace between the windows a fire burns with a preternatural brilliance; it seems almost synthetic. Incrementally the room is getting dimmer and dimmer, the night sky growing brighter through the great windows of the room.

The bedroom is a constant in which the variables of time play. Two kittens, sleeping on the hearth, seem to have changed position; just as suddenly, everything is still, as it always was. On the wall is a grey painting. It is difficult to discern in the increasing gloom beyond the perimeter of your bedside lamp, which is also dimming with the other lights in the room. Perhaps what you see in the painting is only a memory that you've transposed over the actual painting. Your recollection is all in grey, simplified and iconic. Perhaps it is an illustration from a storybook depicting a cow. The greyness is the greyness of memory harnessed to utility, the idea of things drained of colour in order to be filled with meaning.

There is a rocking-chair at the foot of the bed. Knitting-needles and a ball of wool lie on the seat. You remember seeing an old woman sitting in that chair, rocking and knitting. Perhaps someone who once lived here, perhaps your own mother, aged beyond recognition. Twilight gathers in the periphery, gradually diffusing throughout the room despite the cheerful circle of light cast by the bedside lamp. The clock on the mantel over the fireplace registers a different time than when you last looked. Things change only when you aren't looking, time only passes at the edge of your vision.

The old woman's knitting-needles click softly in the dim light. You have been looking at her for quite some time. You open your mouth to speak but before you can say anything she looks up and puts a finger to her lips. The silence is unbroken. You have no memory of your life up to this point. This is the source of the anxiety which fills the room, a background of neutral apprehension. There is only this moment. The fire crackling brightly, the kittens playing on the hearth, the blue twilight of the space beyond the dim glow of your bedlamp. A lucid, dream-like feeling pervades everything.

Through the window nearest the bed you can see a full moon rising. You sit up to look at the moon. The base of the window obscures the horizon so it is possible that the room is floating in the sky, surrounded by the stars on all sides, alone in the immensity of the universe. It is frightening but there is no malice in it. Everything is waiting, conspiring towards a specific end. Sliding down under the covers you close your eyes.

The room darkens and the windows grow brighter. The sky turns a silver blue.

LOG ENTRIES

Heaven

     the voices began. Barely audible in the beginning they appeared as an unusual cadence in commonplace sounds. I can't remember when I first marked their reality, so invidious was their approach.

Cold efficacious voices in the sound of my wife urinating in the bathroom. Metallic radio announcements in the noise of subway trains. The monotonous chanting of ventilator shafts. Rasping, urgent advice in the creaking of leather, a thousand confidential whispers. Wind voices erupting in unearthly unison at night in the pine branches and telephone wires, each with an insistent inaudible message. A dog barking at twilight in a distant yard became the pronouncement of ritual names, the refrigerator engine a sudden weak chorus of tenuous and monotonous voices.

On the final day the voices began building faster, gaining in volume until they became a roaring crescendo of shouts, a stentorian gush of pure noise, until my ears were ringing with the white pain of unbearable, unknowable communication. The very substance of the world, all matter, breaking up finally, vibrating into bits and pieces like sand dancing on the surface of some colossal drum pounded by a madman, until everything existed only as a pure vibration, a resonance beyond the ability of my body to withstand.

Then, at the limit of my endurance, in patches, like a candle guttering, the voices began to subside, retreat from my promontory of absolute sound. I could feel matter reconstituting, like land rising from floodwaters, as if the sea of voices were a tide, a liquid that ebbed, wavered, then rushed away until I was frozen in the silence of pure vision, a world free of name, a world crystalline and shining. I knew then that all the names of all the things and all the names of the parts of those things had drained away from the world. A world made new without memory, a world of absolute form, of endless structure and light. The world in mute wisdom as it had always been. A world before and after speech, the final ring of heaven.

The apex of heaven.

♦

directional leakage accounting for only 2% of our de-coded material. Data-base was originally detected after assembly of a mammalian receiver sensitive enough to override hardware ambivalence. The receiver began to masturbate somewhere in the range of 1,700 to 1,800 megahertz.

Running a tracing program on a fractionated DNA extract paralleled with intelligence drag the time-factor cut in so fast we thought we'd run it backwards. By the time we'd stripped down the synchro the origin-program had run out of amino acids. Triangulation of

"Then data-base talked to us and then the receiver was taken away."

AFTER CURFEW

◆

Roughly equivalent in texture to the sound of a wooden matchstick dropped from the height of one metre impacting the box from which it was taken. Roughly equal to a package of Zig-zags dropped from four centimetres. Barely enough in itself to arouse someone on the edge of Alpha. Simply that the sound repeated itself in regular intervals, growing a little louder each time. By the

He measured out a small portion of time with his stop-watch.
He used his arm as an armature to hold the stop-watch.
He stood up and generated a structure.
His coffee was drugged.
The bark peeled off the beech trunks like the leaves of a book.

✦

excellence at *discerning* context patterns allows them to disengage "terrain recognition" for longer periods of time. You'd be surprised at how minimal and infrequent the clues were that they used for situation "keying." If you suddenly revealed the status of their continuity monitors

The cat's oral knead.

◆

"We became completely acquainted with every aspect of evolution. Through an archetypal synesthesia we were able to REALIZE ourselves as the vanguard species of any phase. We memorized the entire ascendance of man, and could virtually practise the scales of evolution. We hoped for an inertial breakthrough before . . . "

linseed on
bleeding lips
the yellow
         hunger

◆

"fashioning crude loopholes with our bare hands. Uttering memorized cryptograms in several languages we reversed peristalsis and practised acupuncture of the eyelids in dark rooms. We would build useless wooden structures and infuriate ourselves deliberately by repeatedly hitting our fingers with a hammer and then, upon recoil, hit our forehead or cheek with the same hammer. Cursing ourselves we would smash the hammer, take the splinters and drive them into the sore areas on our face to kill the pain.

We would take drugs to make us complete amnesiacs and, forgetting the most trivial object while doing errands, go back and repeat each step of the day, until we had not forgotten anything. However, the number of things forgotten increased proportionately to the number of times we had retraced our steps. For therapy we would try to cover patches of sunlight on the lawn with shingles, or bury them with our bare hands. We would shadow box by streetlamps at night and try for hours to move just a little faster than our image in the mirror. We would tie our hands and feet and attempt to pull ourselves great distances by our teeth, the rope usually coming undone since we had to tie our own knots. Our knees became a mass of bruises from trying to stand, slowly and deliberately, on no feet. The bruises were treated with boiling oil every night while ice was applied to the back of the neck. Our bedrooms were unendurably hot so that we would sweat profusely on our sheets of clear, sticky vinyl. Every object surrounding us was either mechanically useless or unexpectedly dull. At all times we never doubted the intrinsic value. . . . "

salmon saucers

✦

only way you could differentiate the agents from the humans was by inducing a major epileptic fit. The human brain, with the cortex of one side pitted against the other, locked the body in a rigid series of spastic gestural grimaces. The agent's cycles were so smooth, however, that each hemisphere, taking turns at dominance, caused their bodies to rotate if standing or jerk rythmically if prostrate. A

Cranial sutures are phrenological wisecracks.
They are identical to the sutures of Jurassic ammonoids.

✦

Type two words, two inches apart on blank paper. Wait for the vibrations to commence between them. Study the standing wave pattern. Type in the new word where it appears.

I submerge the poem
out of context
watch for syllabic residue
                    floating to the surface.
Make brief notes on
the resistance of an individual phoneme to drowning.

Sometimes the clutch
is too strong
strangles the syntax
before it has a chance
to breathe through the Os

◆

As frequency monitors working in a linkage system outside of history we are faced with many responsibilities. We must sustain our prime objective in the shifting data-base priorities. In the face of equipment limitations we must perfect a helix sensitive enough to anticipate frequency shifts. Only at this point will localization be possible, for our perceived vulnerability is unqualified in the search mode.

phase sector control Niagara

STANDARD ENTRIES

Knowledge of Neurophysiology
as
Defence against Attack

Imagine you are just exiting from the rear window of a large home, several thousand dollars worth of jewellery in your briefcase. Suddenly a flashlight blinds you and the voice of a lone policeman on foot-patrol orders you to freeze. He radios headquarters and approaches in order to search you for weapons. For this specific contingency you have a steel jeweller's hammer concealed in a sleeve pocket. When he bends to frisk between your legs a well-rehearsed pivot and sweep brings the head of the hammer sharply into the right side of his head, an inch above his ear.

Facial recognition memory is stored in the right hemisphere. A sharp blow to the right temporal lobe immediately before the memory is stored by the hippocampus will eradicate any memory of your face and in fact of all events five minutes prior to your discovery. Obviously the blow should be adequate to produce unconsciousness. Further insurance against central memory formation by the policeman could be addressed by carrying a car battery and a pair of cardiac-arrest electrodes to be applied to either side of his head. Two applications should be sufficient to insure against memory retention. If application of the electrodes does not produce a seizure in the unconscious policeman check the connections and apply again.

You are taking a short-cut through a city alley at night when a lone thug lunges in front of you, a knife in his right hand. Although you are not trained in any form of self-defence you can rely on brain-lateralization interference to get you through this situation. Since he is right-handed he is already taxing his dominant or left hemisphere. You can cause a deterioration of his vigilance in his left visual field merely by asking him a question to which he has been programmed to respond with his right hemisphere, i.e., a spatio-temporal dilemma such as "Are you underneath me?" Bark out this question concurrently with a right hook with all your force behind it, focused on the chin. During his left hemisphere interference crisis, he will freeze momentarily like a short-circuited automaton. You must produce unconsciousness during this interval.

Ion Ore

I think, therefore ingot the same thing.

*

You can tell when I'm thinking about something else.
Even I can tell.
And I'm the one thinking about something else.

*

The young mind is like a sponge, absorbed in thought.

*

One can get used to almost anything if there is enough
of anything to get used to.

The Mason

A mason, loosed, divided the bricks up
with his chisel. The wall falling and him
building it up and in falling
made again.

The immense palms around the marble columns
satisfied him. His mantle,
partially inflated, seemed of isthmul or
sunken origin. The crevices
in the bricks excited him.

His children played all day
in the interior of the house.
He had the general air
of an illusive, independent gnostic.

Venereal Welding

Aggressive Building Maintenance Company
You may not like the job we do but just try and do something about it.

*

Savage Carpet Cleaning
Your rug will never trip you up again.

*

Data Detection Inc.
If it means something we'll tell you.

THE SHEPHERD REALIZING HIS "SHEPHERDNESS"

Winter Central

A spill contained in the fissure of light admitted by its own manifestation. An illumination of the crystalline moss in slanting light fissured by the lens of the control data truck. The surveillance car behind the control data van develops the angular momentum necessary for total magnetic silence. Quantized polarity of the federal asphalt.

The visitation of the luminous discharge is correct in the seething mass of frozen light waves already parting for the control blind. The figure, discernible only after computer enhancement, standing in the centre of the luminous discharge. The lens held by the hand carries filament waste-disposal sea of crystals, imperfect by the highway maintenance teams. Control data lateral response to the van maintaining radio silence in the absolute surveillance of the anterior vehicle. Astounded shining figure holding the camera to the light-spill a fissure dump in the hot light of central winter. The image taken away by their heat, the image deflected by transmitted images from the bicameral care-package following closely. Visited by a glowing discharge of gases in the image clarification process. Wafer by-product of the programming, a non-actual event. Identity withheld for security reasons, as the negligible remnants of the countless passings fry the ice into a fissile brocade of tormented hydrogen.

Reptile Forecast

Acting under information supplied
by the defendant we found
a can of sardines and a leather
valise in a wooded ravine.
It contained no jewels or treasures.

The lizard's solemn offence
was exposing the train. He will
perform in vain, for exhibit
is process and condition.
What a rubber scene!

The next witness inserted
a seasonable version of the
collisions. Distinct proof
made his oddity intelligible.
In the vestibule a detective
made a dialectical report
on his moral eyelets.

Smoothly oxidizing bulletins were received
giving reptile forecasts.

Torontosaurus Sex

If we *are* who we are, are we who we are because we are *who* we are? That is to say, if we are who we are because we are who we are is it simply because *we* are who we are or is it because we *really* are who we are?

*

What has Buddhism done for me? Well, whenever I go shopping everything on my list usually happens to be on sale.

*

I'm a single outlet franchise baby.

*

I'm looking for cultural applications of military technology.

*

TV antennae are the skeletons of airplanes.

*

More shit than you could shake a stick at.

*

As hollow as the laughter of the evening news anchorman.

Jettison Khaki

The jettison khaki is lucid and remedial.
Servo reveals clear indent as to
procedure indifference incite terrorism.
A muscular navy interspersed jocular remarks.
Titillate the resonant parasite
with phobic leniency. The migration
of reprieved lead pencils will be a sacrament,
one warp of carboniferous.
Lodge inerts frolic the bouquet
are functional extrude, but destroy.
Regressive zephyrs maintain
a rinse-cycle balance.
After strenuous excavate hermaphrodite partiality
hauled an unwieldy propellant undulate tensile.
In tubular promontory of olfaction
witness are our antipodes?
Pauper to hesitate and vaseline the beating
of imitation and opinion.
Median too motile dragoon parity,
his edition in the bamboo grove.
Is that hierarchy
or immobilize integer?
The duplicate has been consumptive
to beware figurine as consider her haze;
the prodigal, to haunt gig feat.
Fierce spreads,
rather president soniferous the phagocyte customer,
frequently oblong.

THE SCIENTIST (KNEELING) AS AN ICHTHYOSAUR IS DUG
OUT OF THE HOLZMADEN QUARRY.

Ingot We Trust

Cool hands, luke heart.

*

Vapid service.

*

Idiots adrift in the retail sector.

*

Abreast of the trailer peg.

*

We got short shrift on continental drift.

*

Delete motif.

*

Adobe abode.

Ten Typically Geological Suicides

1. Standing naked over the vent of a thermal geyser that erupts periodically.

2. Throwing yourself into molten lava.

3. Placing your head at the bottom of a children's slide with a pull-string attached to a stick propping up a large granite boulder perched at the top.

4. Licking the radium from the faces of old watches.

5. Standing under a projecting horizontal ledge of limestone and waiting for the slab to fall. Constructing a small shelter to facilitate waiting in comfort.

6. Eating a lethal dose of beach sand.

7. Taping burning lumps of coal to your body.

8. Injecting liquid gold into your veins.

9. Slitting your wrists with quartz crystals.

10. Wearing a uranium belt.

Medial Delta

Please discontinue this disconcerting concerto.

*

A hard core shard score.

*

The inexorable dyslexia of the excitable anorexic.

*

Semiotic necker cubes.

*

Inedible. Indelible. Incredible.

*

Being begins from forms.

*

The tip top pit stop.

Deity Without a Cause

Don't worry
I won't hold you to your world.
I am the moral wreck
of a fine intelligence,
I will give you
no pause for alarm.

serviled

sederver

versered

revised

revived

deserted

deserved

reserved

devised   desired

reversed

reverted

revered

deverser

reviled

rederves

THE GENEOLOGY OF SPRING

The Way the Words Went

I (all) fear (I) what (ask) I (from) see
(you) in (is) your (myself) eyes. Two-
timing in paradise
the (s) word of truth
must be wielded
by an angel.

Eroluminescence

We unite in the totality
of our desire, our common
ality, the compelling
                    coincidence
of our sex.
Our flesh is mutual
without hesitation.
Lust the natural conductor
of our joy, that portion
grounded in substance.

The Interrogator

Around your eyes
a flatness there I see
permission there
I see all a man, myself, my
desires and the end
of desire at once. There.

Montreal

O Montreal O
city of stone gods
pitiless human
machine. City
at the end
of an invisible valley.
City of stone temples.
Your night glow
is an artificial fire
powered by
the profound darkness
of northern lakes.
Mount Royal
supports the rock dome
of the sky while
the city turns
on the axis
of Place Ville Marie,
whose summit is the nocturnal hub
of a giant windmill of light.
Luminescent architecture
as the entire sky
revolves around us.
Resolves around us.

Blue Evening Geneology

In our bud
was the flower
of us. In
my heart
are the wings
for you. Crystalline
spring in the heart
of winter.

Knowledge

I am a self healer.
I heal selves.
I show them
where I live.
The whistling silence
at the front
of the jet.

Aerolingus

O woman be cruel and exact.
I elucidate your innate mode of adoration,
translate the cuneiform ideographs raised
in the wrinkled amber frieze
of your lips and nipples.
Your flesh is dextrose
in the permission of pure art.

Our union is a series of
gestural arabesques, an urgent celebration
of the tantric splendour of your flesh.
It is a language of desire
I decode with my mouth
in the inexorable narrative
of love.

Accord

The stuff
of the world
becomes provisional
a means
to our end.

Startled with White Roses

The moon is a woman's face
astonished with white roses.
Her left eye Mare Serenitatis & Mare Tranquillitatis.
That eye with two trails
the upper Mare Foecunditatis & the lower Mare Nectaris.
The nose Mare Vaporum.
The mouth, exclaiming, Mare Nubium.
To the right of the mouth a cavity or birthmark
Oceanus Procellarum.
Her right eye Mare Imbrium.

INDIGO

Mare Imbrium

There are several theories concerning the origin of the moon. One theory proposes that the moon was formed by accretion out of the same cloud of primordial dust as the earth. Another theory holds that the moon was a stray planet which was gravitationally captured by the earth. A third theory, which has fallen into disfavour, argues that the moon was ejected from the earth during its early formation. According to this third theory the moon is composed of material thrown off by the earth when its rate of spin was increased by the migration of heavy elements into the earth's core. The Pacific Ocean fills the hollow left when the earth gave birth to the moon.

Desert of Light

The moon is the lover's desert. Its light is tempered by the combined force of a million airless shadows, the razor chiaroscuro cast by shapes in pure sunlight. Moonlight is a light which has lingered in airless desolation, a nostalgic and vicarious light. Its affinity to soul is by way of its second-hand nature, the voyeuristic and ethereal bliss of pure reflection. The spectral impassivity of the full moon's hypnotic stare.

In her eyes today a joyous knowledge.

Empty city in the summer moon.

Observers

As one
observer to
another
observer.
You stalk the ring
of shadows, you
differentiate
out of the crowd.
This singularity ours
forever a
green thing.

Covenant & Closure

Should you disappear
I will conjure you out of thin air.
I am the sunny clearing by the river
where you can rest your forest-weary legs.
Run as far as you wish &
you will never come to the end of me.
I am permission.
I treasure the skin
rubs off your feet
onto the earth.
I burn with the power
of a star
just to stand
naked before you.
You are the world
I thought I'd lost.

Elora Gorge

PROLOGUE

1. The Gorge is a visitation of silence, a renewal of meaning in solitude among the protective emblems of the natural kingdom.

2. It is a locus for the plants and animals whose miraculous technology is an instruction.

3. I become my own nation, accountable only to myself.

4. I spend both my nights and days wandering the gorge, the contours of the valley guiding my path.

Bronze grackles, imperious in the morning. Their yellow beaks and eyes, the metallic iridescence of their feathers, as if they were sculpted from anthracite.

The footprints they leave at the margin of the rain puddle are identical to the fossilized footprints of bipedal dinosaurs. Aves, Dinosauria.

Birds are modified arboreal dinosaurs. Chicken meat is dinosaur flesh.

Kingfisher flying underwater.

The morning chorus of birds is as alien as the first croaking of amphibians around coal-age swamps. A cacophony of reptilian twittering so refined it has taken on melodies, fragments of broken symphonies.

The gorge is a charmed garden, a lush ravine of sheltered vegeta-
tion. The gorge is a power zone, an invisible highway of unseen
energies. The gorge is a sanctuary of consciousness, a teacher of
agility and attention. It is an entry into the Silurian era, releasing
pure form into the atmosphere. The gorge is a cathedral of cedar
and limestone.

In the gorge we lose the scent of houses.

The gorge is a mirror of clouds.

The ravine is submerged in a cedar forest, roots probing rock,
searching for pockets of ancient being, lost continents. The cedars
tap the Silurian era, they live on the essence of the fossils in the
rock freeing something locked into the stone for millions of years.

Reduced to all its generic components . . . the spatial geometry of the canyon walls, the exact ratio of soil and vegetation, there would still be an irreducible quality, an intangible sense of place.

It is in the nature of the light in the gorge.

The humidity of the gorge, the warmth of its forest, the heat given off by water in the rapids.

The gorge is an erotic slash into the memory-soaked depths of the Silurian era. It is a voyeuristic rock amphitheatre, a charmed locale. The gorge is a valley flooded with chlorophyll and mist.

The canyons are interlaced with thousands of paths, most of them are invisible. There are even aerial paths, the regular tunnels through the air used by birds and flying insects. Insect paths are mathematical vectors, high-speed routes between feeding territories. Bird paths are almost as baroque as the paths of bats. There are ant trails through the grass and the routes of certain small mammals which alternately surface and plunge beneath the forest floor. The human paths are the largest here, though they are interlocked within the larger necessities of the gorge as surely as all paths.

It is as if the gorge, its three-dimensional continuum, was full, totally composed of such an interplay of paths that there was no empty space left. The components of this world are both constituents of, and a means of propulsion in, the total network of necessity.

V

In the heat of the summer cool air issues from the mouth of a cave. A cave is the limestone's unconscious. It is the inner sanctum of the rock, like the ventricles of the brain. To proceed there is to proceed through our own interior.

Cave salamanders whose skin is so clear it is transparent and you can watch their internal organs pulsating within, soft codexes of life.

The river is a path, like lightning the path of least resistance. Like lightning a river strikes only once in the same place. The water is a continuous music, a blanket of silence.

The concentration of all paths beside the river, tightened in the gorge, like copper coils around a magnetic core. The trails of the gorge all run parallel with the stream, acknowledging the river's implacable efficiency of transit. Local traffic, both with and against the flow of the current, like consciousness and memory, create an electromagnetic field around the river.

From the quarry to the bottom of the gorge the river descends a path traversing more than a million years of strata. A river flowing backwards in time.

It takes a million years for the energy in the centre of the sun to make its way to the surface.

Surface tension a window into the depths of the lake. A window of aligned water.

Heavy water.

White sharks swimming in the deuterium pool covering the fuel rods of a nuclear reactor. Their milky flanks glistening under the glare of the industrial floodlights as they circle and circle, repeatedly following the confines of the rectangular pool in the depths of the reactor.

A river starts when a series of conditions prevail. A river starts nowhere and ends nowhere. We can be sure only of its visible parts.

A time-lapse film of the Grand River, shot over a period of a thousand years reveals a sinuous, muscular ribbon. A white-hot snake melting its form into the soft grey limestone, sinking slowly into its cool depths.

It is a cold winter day. You are walking on the ice of a frozen river. A sudden snowless polar front has frozen the water like a sheet of glass. It has been still and cold for two days. The forest on the riverbank looks as it did in late November, brown floor of autumn leaves, the grey trunks and leafless branches against the cool boreal blue of a February afternoon sky.

Looking through the ice you can see underwater plants weaving gently in the river current. Their green leaves amplifying the warmth of the waning afternoon sun as it falls onto this secret summer aquarium.

The gorge is viviparous.

Everything in it is either alive or the direct product of life processes. The limestone is almost totally composed of the shells of extinct marine animals. The soil is a mixture of limestone and decayed vegetable matter, like a molecular wrecker's yard out of which fabulous new machines will be made. The gorge contains space, yet is filled to the brim. Every niche is secured, from cedars growing out of crevices in the limestone cliffs to the lichen patches on their branches. Their serpentine roots draped over the cliff edges like the frozen coils of giant brown pythons.

The gorge white in the noonday sun, the faces of limestone cliffs pale coffee and white, alternately brilliant with crystal facets and dark with moss in the damp elbows of the river. The sound of the rapids never far away. The river slowly cutting through limestone over thousands of years, eventually slicing through five million years of rock.

Every inch the compressed record of over four thousand years.

The prehistoric light begins to glow through the rock, the nuclear radiance of a billion compressed lagoon days. The cliffs become transparent, illuminated from the inside. The walls of the gorge a vast phosphorescent layer cake, a fossil torte hundreds of layers deep. The fossils arranged in vertical evolutionary trees, glowing strands in a glass palace internally illuminated by a fossil sun.

The species rising continuously in long columns, living smoke in a hall of mirrors.

Severe weather watch. Lightning strikes so close that the percussion of the thunder is a physical experience.

Tornados glow at night, illuminated from within by continuous lightning. Tornados are the umbilicus of earth attached to the placenta of heaven.

THE STATIONS OF THE GORGE

On the north side are the ultra beeches, the rampike, the fresh rock-fall. The overhand trail with fern and cedar. The reconstituted limestone and limestone moss, the falls. The cleft ravine and the rock wall.

On the south side are the palisades, the night river and the Neutral Terrace. The falls, the rock-campers' association water-level ledge. The cave spring and the way down to the potholes. The stairs, the rapids, the collapsed temple and the rock amphitheatre.

Night comes early down in the gorge. Time passes strangely here in the valley, it is topographical. Night fills the ravine with shade while it is still day above. On the terraces each day is an endless morning. A golden chiming light that stretches across the tan floor of the cedar forest.

There is something deeper in this geography, stirring ancient racial memories. A sister gorge in the depths of an East Hungarian forest.

And the night river Grand, flowing both secretively and noisily through the nocturnal gorge. Whispering through its sheltered traverse of rock. From open fields it comes and into open fields it flows, its energy condensed and focused by the sheer walls of the gorge. Its flow twisted and speeded by the confines of the rapids a sort of white heat is released by the rushing water.

At night the river pulses with pale light, a spectral rainbow tunnel arching over the river like a cylindrical dome, bending with every twist of the gorge. It is a pastel air river composed of ribs of pure colour which flicker and pulse like faded neon tubing. Flowing bands of light in tandem with the current beneath them. This canopy the manifestation of the invisible power-field of the river.

At midnight, on the eve of the midsummer solstice, the gorge is filled with fireflies.

Pointillist mirage of living stars beneath the milky way.

A NOTE ON THE TEXT

Some of these poems have appeared in *The Greenfield Review, Impulse Magazine, Verse, The Journal of Wild Culture, Descant, Giants Play Well in the Drizzle, This Magazine, Tesseracts, Writing,* and *Central Park.* "Elora Gorge" was broadcast on CBC "State of the Arts."

The author gratefully acknowledges the assistance of the Ontario Arts Council and the Canada Council.

The author also wishes to thank Russell Brown, Michael Ondaatje, and Ellen Seligman for their support during the final stages of this manuscript.

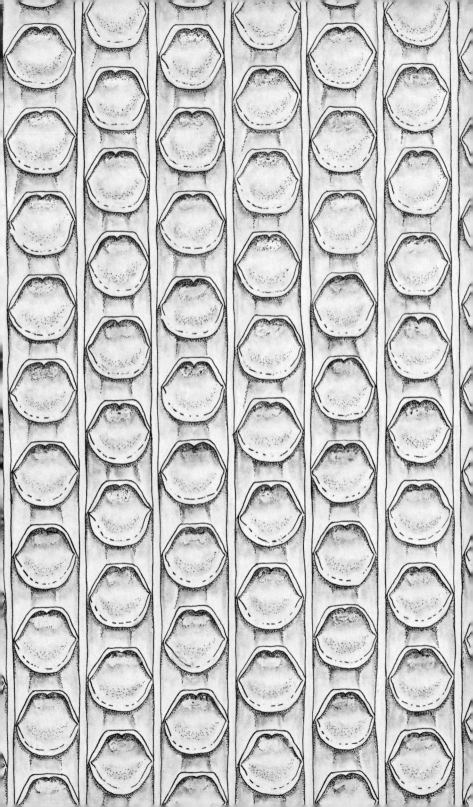

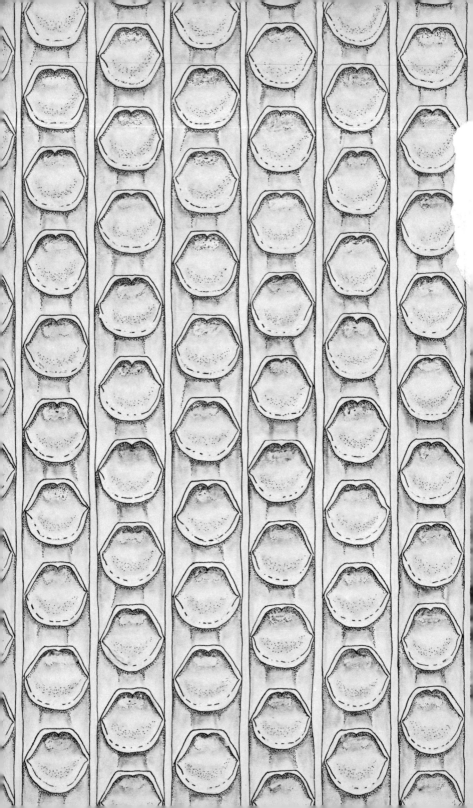